Natural Balance

ESSENTIAL OIL RECIPES
FOR MIND, BODY, & SPIRIT

LAURI HENNINGER

Natural Balance

ESSENTIAL OIL RECIPES
FOR MIND, BODY, & SPIRIT

Columbus, Ohio

Natural Balance : Essential Oil Recipes for Mind, Body, & Spirit
Published by Gatekeeper Press
2167 Stringtown Rd, Suite 109
Columbus, OH 43123-2989
www.GatekeeperPress.com

Copyright © 2020 by Lauri Henninger
All rights reserved. Neither this book, nor any parts within it may be sold or reproduced in any form or by any electronic or mechanical means, including information storage and retrieval systems without permission in writing from the author. The only exception is by a reviewer, who may quote short excerpts in a review.

The cover design, interior formatting, typesetting, and editorial work for this book are entirely the product of the author. Gatekeeper Press did not participate in and is not responsible for any aspect of these elements.

ISBN (paperback): 9781642379198
eISBN: 9781642379204

CONTENTS

Section I: About Essential Oils 9

Benefits Of Essential Oils 11
Essential Oil Properties 12
A Word About Quality 15
Using Essential Oils Safely 17

Section II: Essential Oil Recipes 19

Blending And Usage 21
Roller Bottle Recipes 23

Section III: Yoga, Meditation, & Essential Oils 51

Using Essential Oils For Yoga And Meditation 53
Yoga And Meditation Blends: 54
Chakras And Essential Oils 57
Chakra Blends: 58

INTRODUCTION

My fascination with essential oils began a few years ago. I was reintroduced to oils by a friend, and though I was not a stranger to essential oils, I had very little knowledge about them at the time. When I opened one of the bottles from the small wooden box that she set in front of me, something resonated within me right away. I knew these oils were very different from any I had used in the past.

Through my ongoing interest in these incredible plant essences, I've gained more insight regarding the process of harvesting, growing, and distilling, as well as the reasons why not all essential oils are of equal quality. Pure unadulterated, high-quality essential oils can have a tremendous impact on health and wellbeing; physically, mentally, and spiritually.

As a yoga teacher for more than a decade, a fitness instructor and a Reiki practitioner, I am an advocate for a healthy, holistic lifestyle, particularly when it comes to stress management and emotional wellbeing. Incorporating aromatherapy into my own mind and body practices was a very natural transition for me, and soon after I did so, many of my friends, clients, and students were expressing an interest in essential oils as well.

Aside from being drawn to the captivating scents, I was also intrigued by the effects essential oils seemed to have on my mood, energy, stamina, and emotional state. It didn't take me long to acquire dozens of essential oils and begin researching the chemical constituents and properties they possess, including their benefits and therapeutic value.

It's been about two years since I started experimenting with making my own essential oil blends, and it has been a labor of love. This book is a result of my efforts, and my hope is to provide others with some valuable tools to bring balance and harmony into their lives through the use of these wonderful gifts from nature.

SECTION I

About Essential Oils

BENEFITS OF ESSENTIAL OILS

Essential oils are among the most powerful healing agents found in nature. They offer a range of physical and psychological benefits. The way we feel impacts our overall health. Our thoughts and feelings can influence our choices and habits and set us up for positive or negative experiences, contributing to a lifestyle of wellness, or one of stress-related illness.

Aromatherapy has a profound effect on the mind, and as a result, may influence how we respond in certain situations. Its effects can enhance relationships with others and within ourselves. It can even change our outlook on life by:

- Balancing emotions
- Improving mood
- Instilling confidence
- Reducing anxious feelings
- Relieving stress
- Providing clarity
- Promoting relaxation
- Enhancing health and wellbeing

ESSENTIAL OIL PROPERTIES

Essential oils are highly concentrated compounds extracted from the leaves, stems, roots, needles, bark, fruits and flowers of plants. They are comprised of many aromatic molecules belonging to different chemical groups. These unique combinations of constituents determine their distinctive qualities, including the aroma and therapeutic effects of the oil. Certain oils have uplifting or energizing properties, some have a calming, relaxing effect, and others have soothing or restoring qualities.

The following is a list of those properties and some of the essential oils that exhibit them:

>**Restoring Oils** (strengthen, support, rejuvenate): Frankincense, Cypress, Juniper Berry, Eucalyptus, Rosemary, Cardamom, Siberian Fir, Arborvitae, Helichrysum, Wintergreen, Cinnamon Bark, Cassia, Clove Bud, Lemongrass, Melissa, Cilantro, Thyme, Oregano
>
>**Uplifting Oils** (enliven, inspire, refresh, uplift): Lemon, Lime, Grapefruit, Wild Orange,

Tangerine, Mandarin, Kumquat, Bergamot, Pink Peppercorn, Douglas Fir, Clementine

Energizing Oils (stimulate, motivate, awaken): Peppermint, Spearmint, Fennel, Dill

Calming Oils (relieve stress, relax mind and body): Roman Chamomile, Petitgrain, Bergamot, Clary Sage, Lavender, Magnolia, Coriander, Cilantro, Basil

Soothing Oils (console, reassure, ease emotional and physical issues): Copaiba, Melissa, Black Pepper, Ginger, Cedarwood, Myrrh, Ylang Ylang, Spearmint, Dill, Lemongrass

Clarifying Oils (resolve feelings of uncertainty): Marjoram, Tea Tree, Geranium, Coriander, Cilantro, Basil

Stabilizing Oils (balance emotions, steady the nerves): Patchouli, Cedarwood, Vetiver, Sandalwood, Spikenard, Turmeric

Whether we are smelling essential oils or applying them topically, the molecules enter our bodies within minutes and affect a variety of different systems such as the respiratory, cardiac, muscular systems, as well as our brain and nervous system.

When we breathe in the scent of essential oils our olfactory organs send a message to the limbic system in our brain, including the amygdala—where emotional memories are stored. The limbic system is the area of the brain that governs our emotions. Smell is the only one of the five senses that is directly linked to the limbic lobe of the brain. Feelings such as fear, anger, sadness, anxiousness, and joy all originate from this region.

The olfactory centers of the brain are also directly linked to the hypothalamus, which, along with the pituitary gland, controls physiologic functions throughout the entire body such as heart rate, blood pressure, memory, sleep cycles, stress levels, and hormones.

While different scents can have different effects on the mind and body, studies continue to show that the ancient practice of aromatherapy has true benefits for both physical and emotional concerns.

A WORD ABOUT QUALITY

The quality of essential oils is of utmost importance. Many essential oils on the market are adulterated, meaning they contain contaminants, fillers, and synthetic ingredients. Adulterated or extended oils will not have a predictable therapeutic benefit and may even have harmful physical effects. Inferior quality oils are commonly found on store shelves, including specialty shops and health food stores, and are typically priced much lower than unadulterated, high-quality pure plant oils. Hundreds of companies label their products as 100% Pure Essential Oil, when in fact they contain only trace amounts of essential oil.

For safety and efficacy, it is always best to use essential oils from suppliers who follow strict guidelines for growing, harvesting, distilling, storage, and handling, all factors which can affect the potency of the essential oil. Scientific analysis, preferably GC/MS (Gas Chromatography/ Mass Spectrometry), is the ideal way to ensure the purity and integrity of the essential oil. This analyzes the constituents in oils and can determine if there are any harmful contaminants and fillers, or other plant species present. Most reputable essential oil companies have these tests performed on every batch of oil they receive from their distilleries and provide a way for consumers to easily obtain these batch-specific GC/MS reports. Some of the popular essential oil companies that do this are: doTERRA, Plant Therapy, Rocky Mountain Oils, Edens Garden, and Young Living.

USING ESSENTIAL OILS SAFELY

Essential oils are extremely potent and should be kept out of reach of children and pets. Always dilute essential oils before applying topically to avoid possible skin irritation. Check for sensitivity by applying a small amount to the inside of the wrist. In the event of an adverse skin reaction apply carrier oil to area to further dilute. Do not apply water. Avoid contact with eyes, inner ears, and sensitive areas.

Citrus oils may make the skin more sensitive to ultraviolet light, increasing the risk of sunburn. Avoid going out in direct sunlight for 12-18 hours after applying citrus oils to the skin.

If you are under a doctor's care, pregnant, nursing, or taking medication, consult your physician before using essential oils. Do not ingest them.

For best results, follow the instructions and only use high-quality essential oils from a reputable source when making and using the recipes in this book.

SECTION II

Essential Oil Recipes

BLENDING AND USAGE

Essential oil blends, that is mixtures of pure essential oils, can be quite complex as each essential oil has its own individual character. A well-rounded blend contains a balance of top, middle, and base notes to produce a harmonious and aesthetically pleasing result. Crafting essential oil blends is like an art and can be quite an intuitive and creative process. It involves much experimentation, particularly when blending oils for specific applications.

Carrier oils are oils that are used to dilute essential oils, making them safer for applying to the skin. Carrier oils also allow for better absorption and distribution of the essential oils when used topically. Fractionated coconut oil, sweet almond oil, apricot kernel oil, avocado, and grapeseed oil are some popular carrier oils that are commonly used.

ROLLER BOTTLE RECIPES

The recipes in this book are made with a dilution of 10% essential oil, generally, a safe dilution for healthy teens and adults when used for occasional localized topical application. This equates to approximately 20 drops of essential oil in 10mls of carrier oil. The viscosity, or thickness, varies between oils and therefore this is merely a guideline, as no two drops are exactly the same.

Essential oil roller bottles are relatively easy to find and come in a variety of colors and designs. 10ml is a common size and convenient for on-the-go applications.

To make the roller bottle blends, add the essential oils listed in the recipe to a 10ml glass roller bottle. Fill the bottle the rest of the way with the carrier oil.

The recipes found here call for fractionated coconut oil, abbreviated as FCO for this book, which is a clear, odorless, and widely available carrier oil, however other carrier oils can be substituted. *See the previous section on blending and usage for more suggestions.*

ACCEPTANCE

- 4 drops Grapefruit
- 4 drops Bergamot
- 2 drops Clary Sage
- 5 drops Coriander
- 2 drops Black Pepper
- 3 drops Patchouli
- FCO

The oils of Grapefruit, Black Pepper and Bergamot are excellent for clearing negative self-talk and self-betrayal. Clary Sage oil's reassuring properties assist us when a change of perspective is needed. Patchouli helps stabilize the mind when worry or overthinking takes over, creating peace with ourselves. Coriander oil invites us to reach within our soul and find contentment with who we are. Use this blend to replace judgment and doubt with compassion, worthiness, and self-respect.

ENCOURAGEMENT

- 2 drops Ginger
- 2 drops Eucalyptus
- 1 drop Spearmint
- 8 drops Juniper Berry
- 2 drops Cinnamon Bark
- 5 drops Cedarwood
- FCO

Eucalyptus and Ginger are liberating oils that give us the little boost we need to get us moving. Spearmint works to clear negative energy, enhance mood and concentration, and provide an uplifting lively feeling. Juniper Berry and Cinnamon Bark are beneficial for eliminating fears and insecurities, while Cedarwood provides trust, inner strength, and emotional support. This refreshing blend helps encourage and motivate while instilling a sense of security, stability, and reassurance.

CREATING CALM

- 6 drops Lavender
- 6 drops Bergamot
- 2 drops Roman Chamomile
- 4 drops Cedarwood
- 2 drops Vetiver
- FCO

Lavender is well known for its calming effect and can relieve feelings of depression, stress, and nervous tension. Bergamot, also a very harmonizing oil, improves the vital flow of energy throughout the body and mind, helping to regulate the nervous system. The centering and grounding characteristics of Vetiver and Cedarwood, along with the calming and soothing properties of Chamomile, Bergamot, and Lavender, create a lovely balance of support and release. Relax, unwind, and still the mind and body with this restful blend.

COMMUNICATION

- 6 drops Fennel
- 1 drop Spearmint
- 5 drops Cardamom
- 4 drops Ginger
- 4 drops Sandalwood
- FCO

Fennel oil is beneficial for clearing away mental clutter enabling our thoughts and creativity to be freely expressed. Spearmint oil allows us to communicate with confidence and ease. Sandalwood teaches us to let go of attachments and outdated belief systems. Cardamom oil helps us work through our frustrations in a peaceful, objective manner. Ginger provides a sense of responsibility and ownership of thoughts, words, and actions. This blend encourages us to speak openly and honestly with integrity and self-control.

PATIENCE

- 7 drops Bergamot
- 6 drops Cardamom
- 4 drops Ylang Ylang
- 3 drops Sandalwood
- FCO

Cardamom and Ylang Ylang are uplifting, heart-opening oils that can bring a sense of peace and calm when feeling overburdened and tense. Bergamot's ability to dispel frustration and irritability makes it a great oil for instilling a sense of calm acceptance. Sandalwood promotes stillness, presence, and faith. Find steadiness and comfort with this beautifully balanced blend.

OPENNESS

- 3 drops Eucalyptus
- 3 drops Lavender
- 2 drops Cypress
- 5 drops Wild Orange
- 2 drops Juniper Berry
- 5 drops Cedarwood
- FCO

Eucalyptus encourages us to expand our horizons in order to reduce limiting thoughts, ideas, and behaviors. Cypress and Juniper Berry oils also promote an openness and freedom allowing suppressed feelings to surface and, along with Lavender and Wild Orange, work to unblock stagnant energy. Cedarwood provides strength to navigate through difficulties and helps us resist the powerful emotions that can undermine our confidence and morale. Use this blend to give yourself room to breathe, grow, and adapt to new or challenging situations.

STRESS BUSTER

- 3 drops Vetiver
- 3 drops Ylang Ylang
- 1 drop Frankincense
- 2 drops Clary Sage
- 2 drops Coriander
- 4 drops Wild Orange
- 5 drops Bergamot
- FCO

Vetiver oil brings a sense of calm centeredness and allows us to replenish. Bergamot helps us relax and let go, releasing frustration, tension, irritability. Coriander brings feelings of joy without compromising stability. Together, Wild Orange and Frankincense oils, lift away burdens and help lighten our spirit. Ylang Ylang and Clary Sage oils relax, restore, and promote tranquility. This blend is useful for battling feelings of anxiousness or nervousness, restoring the desire for contentment and helping to reset the emotions.

ANGER MANAGEMENT

- 6 drops Bergamot
- 4 drops Wild Orange
- 4 drops Petitgrain
- 2 drops Roman Chamomile
- 4 drops Ylang Ylang
- FCO

Bergamot oil aids in the processing and releasing of pent-up feelings which can lead to anger and frustration. Ylang Ylang helps us to soften the heart, and, along with Wild Orange, brings joyful optimism, giving us the ability to handle things more smoothly. Roman Chamomile can help soothe feelings of resentment in almost any circumstance, while Petitgrain can be beneficial for building more positive and productive relationships. Cultivate a spirit of calmness, acceptance, and compromise with this very beneficial blend.

CREATIVITY

- 7 drops Tangerine
- 2 drops Neroli
- 4 drops Lemon
- 3 drops Bergamot
- 1 drop Cypress
- 3 drops Frankincense
- FCO

Frankincense and Cypress oils provide inner renewal and open creative channels. The uplifting qualities of Bergamot and Tangerine help us rediscover spontaneity and release the creativity that lies within the spirit. Lemon, along with the sweet floral fragrance of Neroli, eases doubt, invigorates the soul, and fills the heart with hope and joy. This blend can help with creative blockages especially when feeling stuck, rigid, or tense.

MENTAL CLARITY

- 2 drops Rosemary
- 4 drops Clary Sage
- 6 drops Lemon
- 2 drops Peppermint
- 2 drops Juniper Berry
- 4 drops Frankincense
- FCO

Clary Sage and Juniper Berry provide insight and wisdom, allowing us to better organize our thoughts. The invigorating properties of Lemon, Peppermint, and Rosemary work to clear the mind of confusion and mental fog. Frankincense oil's ability to calm and center the mind has a clarifying effect on the intellect. Use this blend to help eliminate distractions and assist with focus, memory, and concentration.

COMPASSION

- 7 drops Wild Orange
- 2 drops Roman Chamomile
- 3 drops Bergamot
- 4 drops Lavender
- 2 drops Helichrysum
- 2 drops Ylang Ylang
- FCO

The oils of Lavender and Ylang Ylang calm and stabilize the heart and allow our emotions to flow. Roman

Chamomile helps with connecting to our true purpose, guiding us toward more fulfilling work. Bergamot and Wild Orange work to instill joy and optimism. The healing properties of Helichrysum restore to the soul its ultimate capacity for kindness toward oneself and others. Dissolve bitterness, heal emotional wounds and open the heart with this soulful blend.

FORGIVENESS

- 3 drops Juniper Berry
- 2 drops Douglas Fir
- 6 drops Bergamot
- 2 drops Copaiba
- 1 drop Thyme
- 1 drop Arborvitae
- 5 drops Myrrh
- FCO

Douglas Fir and Thyme oils assist with letting go of trapped feelings and harmful patterns. Copaiba aids in the release of shame, guilt, bitterness, and hostility. Bergamot is wonderful for helping us let go of self-judgment, allowing us to see the good in ourselves and others. Myrrh and Arborvitae bring forth peaceful surrender, while oil of Juniper Berry fosters a determination to overcome obstacles and guides us toward reconciliation. This blend supports in letting go of negativity and blame toward ourselves or others, allowing us to move forward in peace.

HONESTY

- 6 drops Lavender
- 4 drops Geranium
- 3 drops Black Pepper
- 4 drops Basil
- 3 drops Cassia
- FCO

Lavender oil is beneficial for supporting our mental equilibrium and works well with Geranium and Black Pepper to encourage emotional honesty and personal integrity. Basil oil invites strength and renewal into the heart and helps us break free from negative habits or addictions, restoring our natural rhythms. Cassia assists us in discovering our true gifts and talents so we can live from our authentic Self. This blend is useful in eliminating whatever is holding us back, accessing our emotions, and allowing our true feelings to come to the surface.

WORRY-FREE

- 5 drops Lemon
- 2 drops Grapefruit
- 3 drops Fennel
- 3 drops Clary Sage
- 2 drops Roman Chamomile
- 5 drops Patchouli
- FCO

NATURAL BALANCE

Patchouli oil is very grounding, especially during times of nervousness or excessive worry. Fennel and Chamomile address the feelings associated with overthinking and fixed expectations. Clary Sage oil gives us the ability to trust our instincts, clear the mind, and clarify our spiritual vision. The citrus oils of Lemon and Grapefruit are refreshing, cleansing, and uplifting. Use this blend to calm the nervous system, and feel more balanced, restored, and at ease.

JOYFULNESS

- 5 drops Tangerine
- 5 drops Green Mandarin
- 2 drops Petitgrain
- 4 drops Bergamot
- 1 drop Clove Bud
- 1 drop Ylang Ylang
- 2 drops Sandalwood
- FCO

Green Mandarin and Tangerine oils promote a cheerful, positive disposition, and together with Bergamot, can lift and stabilize our mood. Petitgrain has the ability to calm and uplift and clear out negative emotions that keep us bound. Clove Bud oil reignites the soul, while Ylang Ylang helps reconnect us to the joyful innocence of our childhood. Sandalwood oil works to replace obsessive overthinking with spiritual clarity. Cultivate feelings of happiness and joy with this calming, uplifting blend.

CENTERED

- 6 drops Vetiver
- 4 drops Cardamom
- 2 drops Marjoram
- 8 drops Lemon
- FCO

Cardamom helps to relax us, firm our resolve, and restore feelings of contentment. Together Cardamom and Vetiver oils work to strengthen, support and stabilize. Marjoram along with Cardamom restores balance to the nervous system, and Lemon oil helps us stay present, focused, and mentally connected. This beautifully balanced blend can help us release feelings of overwhelm, frustration, and disconnect, and become more grounded and present in all areas of life.

ADAPTABILITY

- 8 drops Wild Orange
- 2 drops Cinnamon Bark
- 3 drops Siberian Fir
- 3 drops Rosemary
- 4 drops Frankincense
- FCO

Wild Orange oil brings spontaneity, renews energy, and aids with life's transitions, and Siberian Fir assists us whenever we are experiencing a major change. Frankincense helps to lift the weight of over-attachment while providing guidance and protection. Cinnamon Bark oil offers assurance during times of uncertainty, and Rosemary opens us up to new experiences. This supportive blend helps ease difficult transitions, encouraging acceptance and appreciation.

FINDING PASSION

- 8 drops Lime
- 5 drops Ginger
- 3 drops Black Pepper
- 3 drops Ylang Ylang
- 1 drop Cinnamon Bark
- FCO

Lime oil refreshes and cheers the heart, bringing out encouragement and a zest for life. Ginger oil persuades us to participate and be present. Black Pepper and Cinnamon Bark support emotional honesty with ourselves and others, and Ylang Ylang brings freedom, joy, and playfulness back to the heart. This wonderful, exotic blend can help instill feelings of pleasure and happiness, reigniting our passion for life.

RESTORATION

- 4 drops Coriander
- 4 drops Litsea or Lemongrass
- 4 drops Grapefruit
- 1 drop Geranium
- 2 drops Black Pepper
- 5 drops Vetiver
- FCO

The refreshing, uplifting qualities of Coriander oil instill optimistic and inventive resourcefulness. Litsea, as well as Lemongrass oil, is healing and cleansing to the soul, and Grapefruit oil helps lighten and revitalize the spirit. Geranium restores a sense of love and trust to the heart and heals emotional wounds. Vetiver reassures and reconnects, helping us to identify the root of emotional issues. Black Pepper oil also gives us the strength to overcome personal challenges by releasing trapped feelings. Use this blend to combat nervous exhaustion or feelings of despair or apathy.

CONFIDENCE

- 3 drops Green Mandarin
- 3 drops Wild Orange
- 4 drops Bergamot
- 3 drops Ginger
- 3 drops Cinnamon Bark
- 4 drops Sandalwood
- 5ml FCO

Bergamot and Cinnamon Bark oils encourage the release of self-doubt and insecurity. Sandalwood oil keeps us connected to our inner light, while Wild Orange and Green Mandarin allow that light to shine forth. Ginger promotes feelings of empowerment, responsibility, and commitment. Let go of limiting beliefs, seek to achieve your full potential, and trust in Divine guidance with this wonderful blend.

STRENGTH AND ENDURANCE

- 3 drops Arborvitae
- 6 drops Peppermint
- 6 drops Wild Orange
- 3 drops Clove Bud
- 2 drops Rosemary
- FCO

Arborvitae oil provides the stability and support that enables us to balance effort with ease. Clove Bud gives us the strength needed to stand up for ourselves while protecting our boundaries. Peppermint and Wild Orange revitalize, offering positive energy, optimism, and renewal, and Rosemary oil's boldness helps us realize our full potential. Reach for this blend when you need a boost of energy, courage, or stamina.

RESPONSIBILITY

- 5 drops Fennel
- 4 drops Ginger
- 3 drops Cardamom
- 6 drops Lime
- 2 drops Cassia
- FCO

Fennel and Ginger are oils that help with motivation including the ability to respond and take action. Cardamom eases feelings of frustration and blame, providing mental stability and self-control. Cassia gives us the courage to try new things, especially when plagued with the fear of failure. Lime oil is a great motivator as it reveals our inner motives and instills determination when we'd rather retreat. Use this blend to assist in taking ownership and responsibility for choices and actions.

COMFORT

- 2 drops Geranium
- 4 drops Lime
- 2 drops Tangerine
- 2 drops Marjoram
- 4 drops Frankincense
- 6 drops Ylang Ylang
- FCO

Geranium, Marjoram, and Ylang Ylang are powerful remedies for the brokenhearted. Tangerine and Lime work to uplift and lighten the heart, providing hope and encouragement during difficult times. Frankincense oil helps with our spiritual evolution, lighting our way and providing new perspectives. Begin to heal the heart, let go of sadness or grief, and move forward in peace with this healing, supportive blend.

HARMONY

- 5 drops Frankincense
- 4 drops Petitgrain
- 7 drops Bergamot
- 3 drops Marjoram
- 1 drop Cinnamon Bark
- FCO

Frankincense oil provides a pathway to the soul, opening spiritual channels. Petitgrain oil supports us in finding balance and alignment with our true self. Bergamot instills emotional contentment by allowing us to better process our feelings. Cinnamon Bark oil also supports the clearing of trapped emotions, and Marjoram oil invites feelings of happiness and equanimity, creating a sound mind and body. Invoke feelings of joy, peace, and contentment with this lovely, balancing blend.

BODY CONTENTMENT

- 8 drops Grapefruit
- 3 drops Ginger
- 2 drops Cassia
- 5 drops Cardamom
- 2 drops Patchouli
- FCO

Grapefruit oil helps bring about approval and kindness towards ourselves, and especially in honoring and loving our bodies. Cassia also encourages respect and love for ourselves, and Ginger oil provides support when feeling defeated. Cardamom oil helps with releasing emotional distortions, and Patchouli assists us in finding peace in our physical body, appreciating its magnificence and eliminating judgment. This blend encourages acceptance, awareness, and responsibility while instilling self-love.

COURAGE

- 2 drops Lavender
- 2 drops Cypress
- 2 drops Juniper Berry
- 2 drops Black Pepper
- 3 drops Cassia
- 7 drops Lime
- 2 drops Helichrysum
- FCO

NATURAL BALANCE

Lime oil, as well as Black Pepper oil, provide the hope, determination, and courageousness needed to face life's challenges. Lavender assists us in helping express ourselves openly with confidence. Cypress invites us to get out of our own way and allow life to flow freely. Juniper Berry encourages us to address our fears, and Cassia oil is a wonderful remedy for the shy, timid individual. Helichrysum restores faith, giving us the strength to carry on despite past difficulties. This is a great blend for building personal value, determination, and bravery.

AUTHENTICITY

- 5 drops Wild Orange
- 5 drops Frankincense
- 4 drops Cassia
- 4 drops Black Pepper
- 2 drops Spearmint
- FCO

Frankincense oil helps us break free of attachment and connect with our inner truth. Wild Orange invites us to let go and live like we did as a child with playfulness, humor, and spontaneity. Spearmint oil brings clear thought and expression, and Black Pepper and Cassia encourage us to come out of hiding and live honestly and truthfully. This powerful blend can assist us in opening up to new and higher perceptions, allowing our true self to emerge.

TENSION TAMER

- 3 drops Marjoram
- 3 drops Spearmint
- 3 drops Peppermint
- 2 drops Wintergreen
- 2 drops Basil
- 4 drops Siberian Fir
- 1 drop Blue Tansy
- 2 drops Frankincense
- FCO

Marjoram and Siberian Fir have very soothing and calming qualities. Basil oil's revitalizing action assists us when suffering from physical or mental fatigue and, together with Frankincense provides relief from nervous exhaustion. Peppermint and Blue Tansy also support us in relieving physical and emotional pain, and Spearmint can help dissolve tension, stress, and emotional blockages. Wintergreen oil allows us to surrender our burdens, lifting the weight off our shoulders. This blend helps us feel rejuvenated physically, mentally, and spiritually.

EMPOWERMENT

- 4 drops Ginger
- 2 drops Clove Bud
- 2 drops Arborvitae
- 4 drops Fennel
- 3 drops Cinnamon Bark

NATURAL BALANCE

- 🖐 5 drops Tangerine
- 🖐 FCO

Tangerine oil brings forth a creative energy flow while Fennel and Ginger both provide a willingness to get us moving and take action. Cinnamon Bark releases us from fear of rejection, while Clove Bud encourages us to set boundaries, yet remain proactive, regardless of the opinions of others. Arborvitae oil helps us find strength and stability while at the same time allowing us the ability to relinquish excessive struggle or control. Use this blend to promote independence and ownership of choices, and to let go of victim mentality.

ATTITUDE ADJUSTMENT

- 🖐 4 drops Copaiba
- 🖐 4 drops Litsea Cubeba (May Chang)
- 🖐 3 drops Black Pepper
- 🖐 2 drops Cassia
- 🖐 5 drops Ylang Ylang
- 🖐 2 drops Frankincense
- 🖐 FCO

Copaiba and Black Pepper help soothe anxiety and expose unresolved pain and suppressed emotions. Litsea Cubeba, also known as May Chang oil is very cleansing and healing, and beneficial for removing stagnant energy. Ylang Ylang allows us to release pent up emotions and regain our sense of trust. The use of Frankincense and Cassia oils date back to biblical times and bring gladness and courage to the soul, support healthy immunity, and instill spiritual calmness. Reach for this blend to turn negative feelings into positive ones, help switch your perspective, and create a brighter, healthier outlook.

PURPOSEFULNESS

- 4 drops Roman Chamomile
- 4 drops Ginger
- 1 drop Cassia
- 2 drops Black Pepper
- 6 drops Red Mandarin
- 3 drops Jasmine
- FCO

Roman Chamomile helps us find purpose and meaning in our lives, and Cassia oil assists us in revealing our own gifts and talents. Black Pepper unveils our feelings and motives and invites us to live a life of integrity, truthfulness, and authenticity. Ginger oil helps us put our thoughts and ideas into action, and become the creator of our destiny. Red Mandarin brings forth feelings of joy, contentment, and motivation, and Jasmine oil restores the true desires of the soul. This blend can help us develop determination, intention, and initiative to discover and live our life's true purpose.

CALM FOCUS

- 4 drops Vetiver
- 9 drops Wild Orange
- 3 drops Peppermint
- 2 drops Cedarwood
- 2 drops Lavender
- FCO

Vetiver can help with centering, especially for individuals who have difficulty with being easily distracted. Peppermint oil, especially when combined with Wild Orange, boosts mood and brain function. Lavender and Cedarwood oils are calming and soothing to the central nervous system and work together to reduce anxious feelings. This is a very beneficial blend for those who are easily excitable, have a short attention span, or difficulty concentrating and staying on task.

INSPIRATION

- 9 drops Wild Orange
- 3 drops Laurel Leaf
- 4 drops Ginger
- 2 drops Peppermint
- 2 drops Coriander
- FCO

Wild Orange works to promote a cheerful attitude and an energized mood. Laurel Leaf helps to dispel doubt and spark intuition and creativity. Ginger oil ignites our inner fire, eliminating feelings of complacency or helplessness. Peppermint oil is particularly valuable during times of depression or despair, assisting us in working through issues that are holding us back. Coriander takes us out of our comfort zone as we learn to let go of our need for approval from others and find our own truth. Use this blend to enliven the senses, provide insight, and awaken new possibilities.

BELONGING

- 5 drops Cedarwood
- 1 drop Arborvitae
- 2 drops Birch or Wintergreen
- 2 drops Cinnamon Bark
- 2 drops Siberian Fir
- 8 drops Wild Orange
- FCO

Cedarwood and Siberian Fir oils bring feelings of certainty, support, and connection. Arborvitae oil reminds us that we are always loved and supported and invites us to release struggle and control. Birch oil also brings support, grounding, and centering qualities. Cinnamon Bark helps us to address our insecurities, while Wild Orange encourages us to enjoy all the abundance around us. Reach for this blend to combat feelings of alienation, seclusion, or loneliness.

TRUST

- 2 drops Geranium
- 1 drop Arborvitae
- 2 drops Cypress
- 4 drops Coriander
- 7 drops Bergamot
- 4 drops Myrrh
- FCO

Geranium helps those who have lost hope in people and the world around them to regain a sense of trust. Coriander oil assists in processing emotions related to fears of the heart. Arborvitae helps us to ease up and release the need to be in complete control of every situation. Cypress provides emotional grounding and, together with Bergamot oil, encourages us to flow with life. Myrrh helps to heal relationships and rekindle trust within the soul. A wonderful blend to promote openness, integrity, and eliminate feelings of betrayal so that we can learn to trust again.

REJUVENATION

- 4 drops Frankincense
- 9 drops Bergamot
- 2 drops Siberian Fir
- 2 drops Basil
- 3 drops Coriander
- FCO

Bergamot oil supports us in letting go of negative thinking, releasing tension and stress. Frankincense helps with improving our attitude by letting go of deception and negativity. Basil is great for renewing the mind and restoring energy and vitality. Coriander helps us find the joy that we have lost in our life, and Siberian Fir is wonderful for letting go of regrets or negative associations to the past. This blend relaxes the senses bringing a balanced renewal, stable energy, and a positive outlook.

EMOTIONAL REBOOT

- 2 drops Rosemary
- 6 drops Petitgrain
- 2 drops Copaiba
- 4 drops Douglas Fir
- 6 drops Wild Orange
- FCO

Rosemary oil is beneficial for during times of transition, supporting changes in perspective and deepening our understanding. Petitgrain, a potent mood elevator, helps us release negativity and see the brighter side of every situation. Copaiba works to reset and balance our whole system, and Douglas Fir oil helps us break free of destructive patterns and encourages new pathways. Wild Orange instills positive attitude, helping us to proceed with a more relaxed approach. This blend is beneficial for resetting, transitioning, or clearing out dysfunctional habits.

GRATEFUL HEART

- 2 drops Spikenard
- 1 drop Frankincense
- 2 drops Myrrh
- 2 drops Geranium
- 5 drops Ylang Ylang
- 8 drops Wild Orange
- FCO

Spikenard oil encourages us to live in gratitude for all we have in life, while Wild Orange reminds us of our limitless abundance. Geranium and Ylang Ylang, the heart-healing oils, open us up to appreciation and acceptance. Frankincense and Myrrh helps us to feel loved, inviting in feelings of peacefulness and tranquility, and assisting us in our spiritual evolution. Use this uplifting blend any time you need a gentle reminder to be thankful for all of the goodness in your life.

SECTION III

Yoga, Meditation, & Essential Oils

USING ESSENTIAL OILS FOR YOGA AND MEDITATION

Aromatic essences have been used for centuries in many types of spiritual practices. They can provide a wonderful complement to your personal yoga or meditation practice as they each have the ability to transform, heal, and work to create a more meaningful connection with something bigger than ourselves. Combining the ancient practices of yoga and aromatherapy allows for healing on emotional, physical, and spiritual levels. Bringing the earthly element of plants and nature into our spiritual practices, can enhance our overall experience by helping us recognize the natural balance that is occurring all around us, always.

The following essential oil roller bottle blends can be applied topically to the forehead, chest, back of the neck or ankles, or to pulse points such as inner wrists, inner elbows, behind the ears, before or during your yoga or meditation practice. The oils usually take effect within just a few minutes of application.

YOGA AND MEDITATION BLENDS

MINDFULNESS

- 5 drops Vetiver
- 3 drops Lavender
- 2 drops Frankincense
- 3 drops Marjoram
- 5 drops Ylang Ylang
- 1 drop Clary Sage
- 1 drop Spearmint
- FCO

This blend helps provide clarity, insight, and connectedness for a calm and centered yoga and meditation practice.

PRESENCE

- 2 drops Patchouli
- 2 drops Vetiver
- 3 drops Black Pepper

NATURAL BALANCE

- 2 drops Fennel
- 11 drops Kumquat
- FCO

This yoga blend helps us stay grounded and centered in truth, authenticity, and awareness. Perfect for a physically active or vinyasa style yoga practice coupled with a quiet, reflective meditation.

AWAKENING

- 5 drops Frankincense
- 3 drops Rosemary
- 3 drops Spearmint
- 5 drops Lemon
- 4 drops Clary Sage
- FCO

A wonderful blend to lighten, brighten, and uplift the senses, raise our vibrations and reveal our inner truth. Great for all types of yoga and meditation practices.

REST AND RENEW

- 5 drops Green Mandarin
- 4 drops Cardamom
- 2 drops Fennel
- 3 drops Coriander
- 3 drops Ginger
- 1 drop Clove Bud

- 2 drops Sandalwood
- FCO

This blend of oils helps bring the body and mind into a state of balance and equanimity. It is a wonderful blend for restorative yoga practices when the ultimate goal is to rest and relax.

PEACE AND TRANQUILITY

- 6 drops Lavender
- 4 drops Patchouli
- 4 drops Vetiver
- 3 drops Sandalwood
- 3 drops Spikenard
- FCO

This blend helps instill a profound feeling of peacefulness, wholeness, and contentment. A great calming blend for savasana and guided meditations.

CHAKRAS AND ESSENTIAL OILS

"Chakra", the Sanskrit word for "wheel", refers to the energy centers of the subtle body, most notably the seven primary centers located along the spine from the base through the crown of the head. How we feel on an emotional level is related to our chakra system. Our thoughts, feelings, and attitudes can influence the energy flow at these centers. When one or more of our chakras are out of balance this can affect our whole system. When all the chakras are spinning at the proper vibrational frequencies, there is harmony physically, mentally, and spiritually.

The chakra blends were created to support and balance the chakras. They are great for yoga classes or anytime you wish to address a specific chakra. They can be applied topically or added to an essential oil diffuser. If you choose to use them in a diffuser, add half the number of drops of the essential oils listed in the recipe and omit the carrier oil. Be sure to diffuse in an open area or well-ventilated room.

CHAKRA BLENDS

GROUNDING

Root Chakra – *Muladhara*

Affirmation: I am strong, healthy, and secure in body and soul.

- 4 drops Vetiver
- 6 drops Cedarwood
- 2 drops Arborvitae
- 2 drops Lemon Eucalyptus
- 6 drops Lavender
- FCO

An unbalanced root chakra can produce feelings of insecurity, fear, confusion, and depression. This blend provides stable, grounding, protective properties and calms the central nervous system, cultivating feelings of vitality, wellness, and connectedness.

CREATIVE ENERGY

Sacral Chakra – *Svadhisthana*

Affirmation: I approach life with passion and exuberance.

- 4 drops Tangerine
- 6 drops Sandalwood
- 4 drops Bergamot
- 2 drops Cinnamon Bark
- 4 drops Fennel
- FCO

Problems associated with the sacral chakra include low energy, creative blocks, lack of motivation, and often times addictions. This blend encourages optimism, creativity, and joy of life. It helps connect the body and the self.

SELF-ASSURANCE

Solar Plexus Chakra – *Manipura*

Affirmation: My personal integrity, confidence, and self-esteem increase with each day.

- 4 drops Marjoram
- 8 drops Coriander
- 4 drops Wild Orange
- 2 drops Cassia
- 2 drops Ginger
- FCO

When there are imbalances of the solar plexus chakra, we can feel worthless, powerless, and self-critical, as well as nervous and anxious. This blend supports individual choice, confidence, trust, and determination while asking us to honor and live from the true self.

EMOTIONAL BALANCE

Heart Chakra – *Anahata*

Affirmation: A calm inner peace fills my mind and body.

- 2 drops Roman Chamomile
- 8 drops Green Mandarin
- 4 drops Patchouli
- 4 drops Ylang Ylang
- 2 drops Geranium
- FCO

Low energy in the heart chakra can show up as anger, bitterness, melancholy, and jealousy or envy. This blend lightens and heals the heart, promotes forgiveness and trust, and works to connect the upper and lower chakras.

EXPRESSION

Throat Chakra – *Vishuddha*

Affirmation: My words and actions inspire me and those around me.

- 2 drops Basil
- 2 drops Lavender
- 4 drops Spearmint
- 4 drops Fennel
- 4 drops Ginger
- 2 drops Eucalyptus
- 2 drops Clove Bud
- FCO

The throat chakra relates to how we express our truth, communicate our needs, and move toward manifesting our desires. This blend offers a sense of renewal and opens us up for confident verbal expression while maintaining responsible boundaries.

INSIGHT

Third Eye Chakra – *Ajna*

Affirmation: I observe my emotions without getting attached to them.

- 4 drops Clary Sage
- 4 drops Lemon

- 2 drops Juniper Berry
- 2 drops Peppermint
- 4 drops Cardamom
- 4 drops Sandalwood
- FCO

The third eye chakra addresses our inner vision and perspective. It affects our ability to determine between truth or illusion. This blend quiets the mind and aids in spiritual progress, dispelling confusion and providing insight and clarity.

ENLIGHTENMENT

Crown Chakra – *Sahasrara*

Affirmation: I transcend stress of any kind. I live in peace.
- 2 drops Frankincense
- 2 drops Myrrh
- 2 drops Cypress
- 6 drops Wild Orange
- 4 drops Ylang Ylang
- 4 drops Bergamot
- FCO

The crown chakra represents complete integration, unity, and oneness. It connects us to the divine and aligns us beyond words or intellect. This blend inspires peace and tranquility, shows us how to instill perfect trust in the flow of life, and to live in the moment.

www.ingramcontent.com/pod-product-compliance
Lightning Source LLC
LaVergne TN
LVHW051226070526
838200LV00057B/4628